Creative Keyboard

MW01675511

Great Literature for Piano

Baroque – Classical – Romantic

BOOK VIII
MUSICALLY ADVANCED

Researched and Compiled by

GAIL SMITH

Creative Keyboard Publications MEL BAY

Foreword

In early 19th-century Germany, the purchase of a piano commanded the interest of the new owner's entire community. The German family that ordered the piano first made a down-payment in cash. Upon completion of the piano, they paid for the balance in corn, wheat, potatoes, poultry, and firewood.

On the day that the piano was to be delivered to the new owner, the town held a festival. A band of musicians headed the procession, followed by the proud piano maker, who was borne on the shoulders of his assistants. Flowers and wreaths decorated the horse-drawn wagon which held the precious piano. Musicians, schoolmasters, and dignitaries marched in the rear.

At last the piano arrived at its destination. The delighted new owners greeted the procession warmly. The local clergyman said a prayer, blessing the new instrument as well as its craftsmen. The mayor delivered an address; the schoolmaster, doctor, and other dignitaries gave speeches. Finally, the men's chorus sang. When the piano was properly installed in its new home, everyone enjoyed a banquet and danced in celebration of this happy occasion.

In contrast, today the purchase of a piano seems no longer to be a cause for festivity and joy. Unfortunately, our generation takes such purchases for granted. We have forgotten what a treasure and gift a piano can be. We have also forgotten what a treasure and gift the great composers have given us through their beautiful musical compositions for the piano.

This new piano literature series rediscovers the "rare jewels" of piano literature. After years of research and meticulous assessment of the composers of Baroque, Classical, and Romantic music, this exciting "quest for the best" has led to a new series of eight graded books . . . all containing original compositions by the masters.

The series begins with the most easily mastered compositions, progressing to the more advanced and musically difficult selections. Pianists on all levels will enjoy this challenging, thorough, and diversified collection of piano music. In addition, an interesting biographical sketch of each composer will make these selections more meaningful to the student.

Just as flowers and wreaths decorated the horse-drawn wagon that delivered the new piano to the fortunate German villager, likewise flowers and wreaths decorate each book in this series. They serve as a reminder for us all to treasure each selection we learn and to be thankful for our magnificent musical heritage.

Gail Smith

Note to Teachers

The pieces selected in each book are in approximate order of difficulty. They are not necessarily in chronological order. Before the selections of each new composer, there is a short biographical sketch of that composer. In addition, many include a pictorial representation, as well.

Book One . . . . late primary-level and early elementary-level pieces

Book Two . . . . harder elementary pieces

Book Three . . . . medium-level or intermediate pieces

Book Four . . . . difficult pieces

Book Five . . . . more difficult pieces

Book Six . . . . very difficult pieces

Book Seven . . . . musically advanced sonatas

Book Eight . . . . musically advanced longer pieces

Contents
Book Eight

Chromatic Fantasia and Fugue . . . . Johann Sebastian Bach 9

Papillons (Op. 2) . . . . Robert Schumann 37

Rhapsodie in G minor (Op. 79, No. 2) . . Johannes Brahms 60

Variations Sérieuses (Op. 54) . . . . Felix Mendelssohn 72

Premiére Ballade (Op. 23) . . . . Frederic Chopin 95

Fantaisie - Impromptu (Op. 66) . . . . Frederic Chopin 116

Les Huguenots (Op. 20) . . . . Sigismond Thalberg 130

Johann Sebastian Bach

(March 21, 1685 – July 28, 1750)

The "Chromatic Fantasia and Fugue" is the most famous single piece that Bach composed. No words can describe the Fantasia. It sounds as if Bach were sitting down playing one of his inspired improvisations. The fugue is a masterpiece by the inventor of the fugue himself. The fugue begins with one voice coming in like a little stream. Then another voice joins in making harmony, yet carrying its own story. Then a third voice like a river enters the sea of notes to carry its message. Miraculously the trinity of tones harmonize, united in perfect form, creating poetry in music of the highest order.

Chromatic Fantasia and Fugue

Johann Sebastian Bach

p
p
cresc.
poco
a poco
Ped.
Ped.
f
p
cresc.
f
mf
p
cresc.
f
R.H.
L.H.

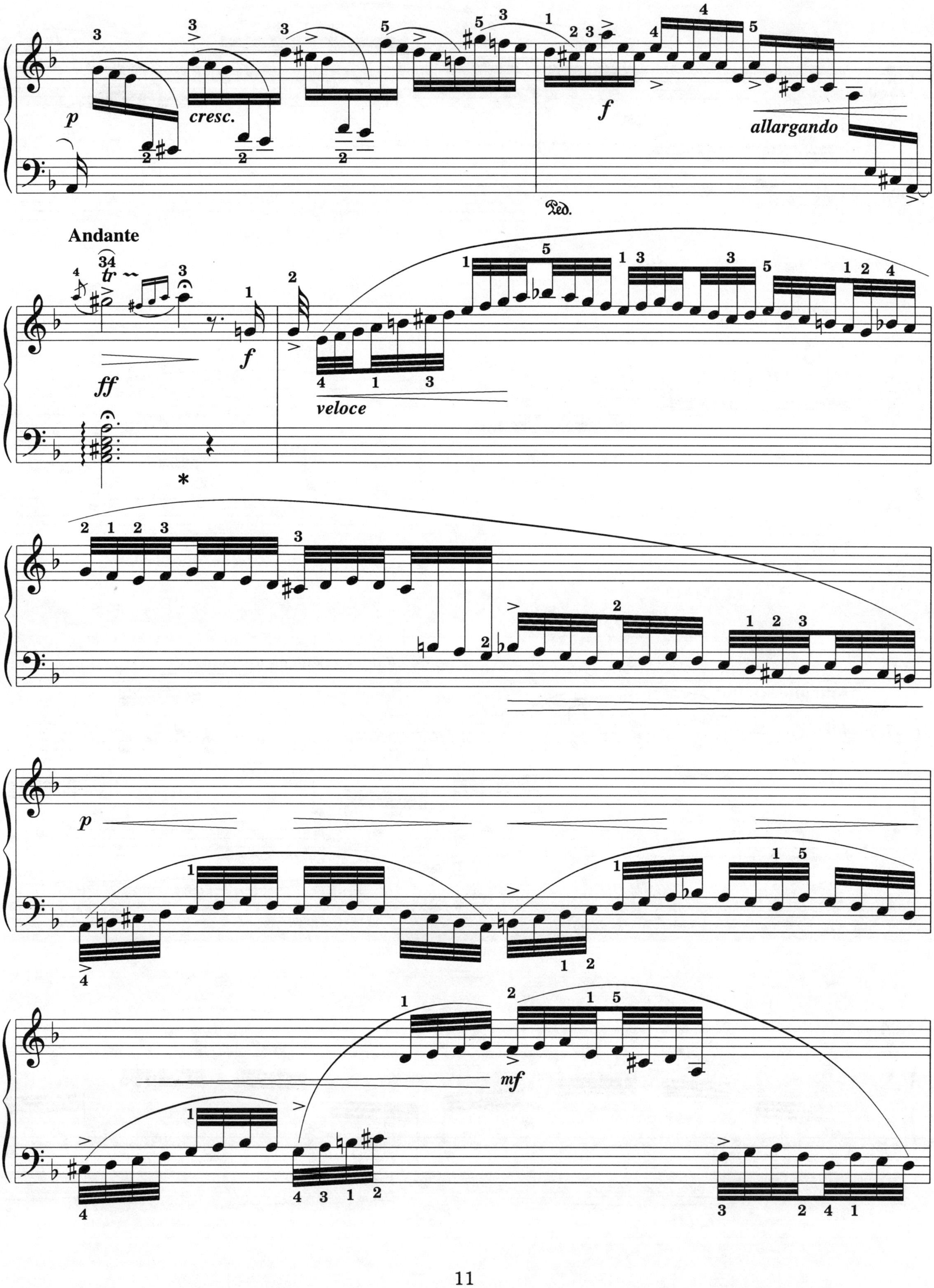

p
cresc.
f
allargando
Ped.
Andante
tr
ff
f
veloce
p
mf

f rallent.
dim.
Andante sciolto
p
poco a poco cresc. ed animandosi
Ped.

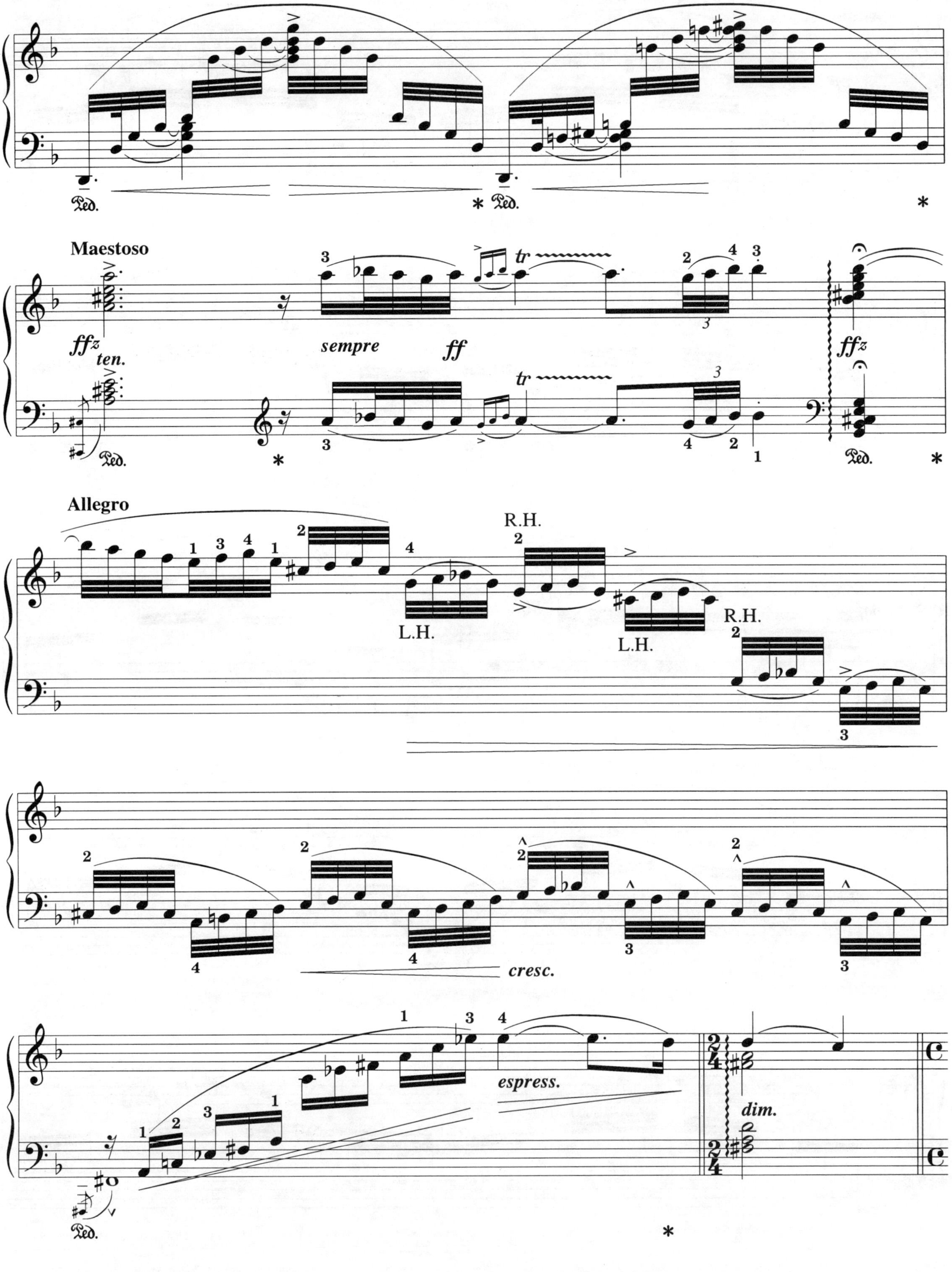
Ped.
Maestoso
ffz
ten.
sempre
ff
tr
Allegro
R.H.
L.H.
cresc.
espress.
dim.

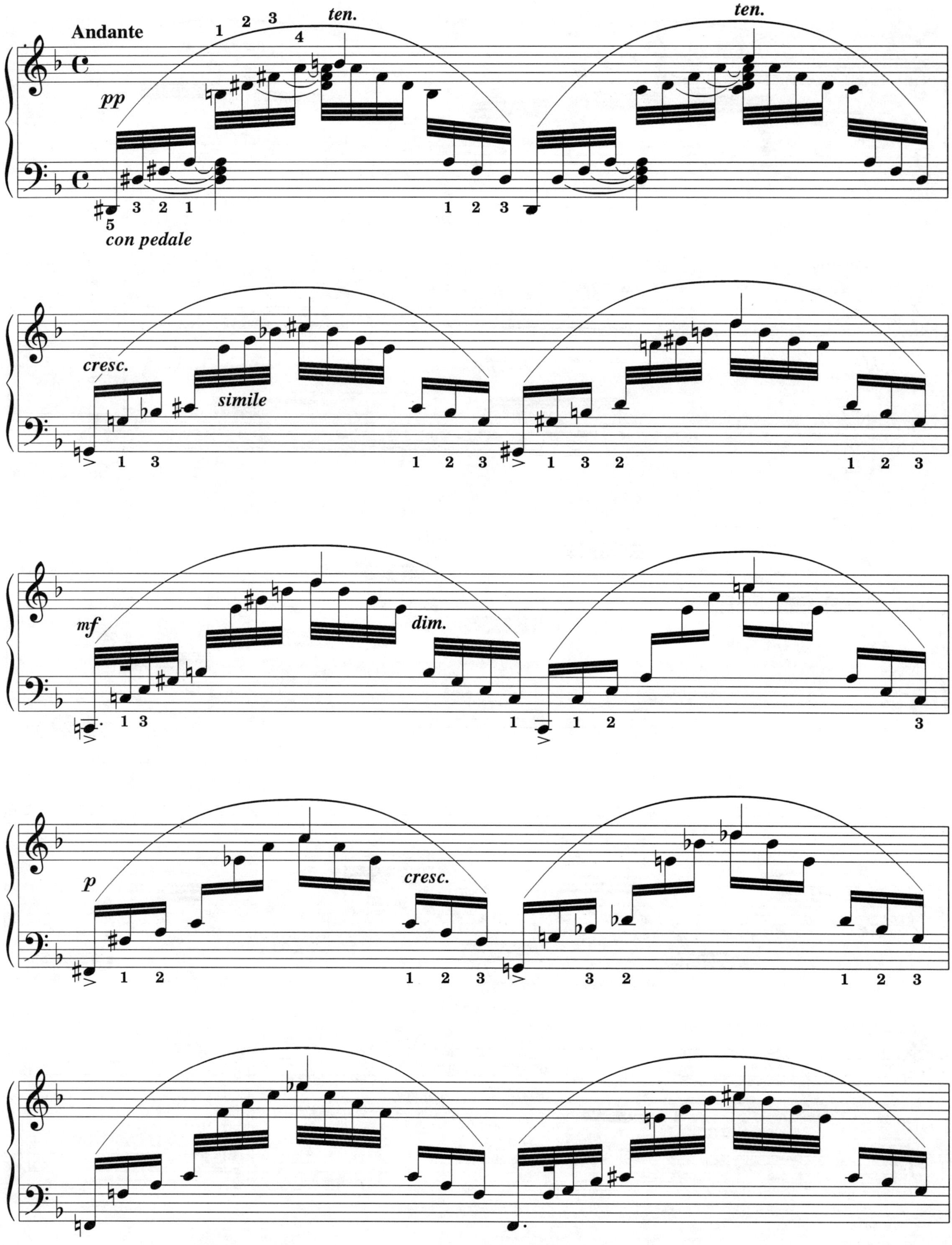
Andante
ten.
ten.
pp
con pedale
cresc.
simile
mf
dim.
p
cresc.

f
ff rallent.
Ped.
dim.
ten.
espress.

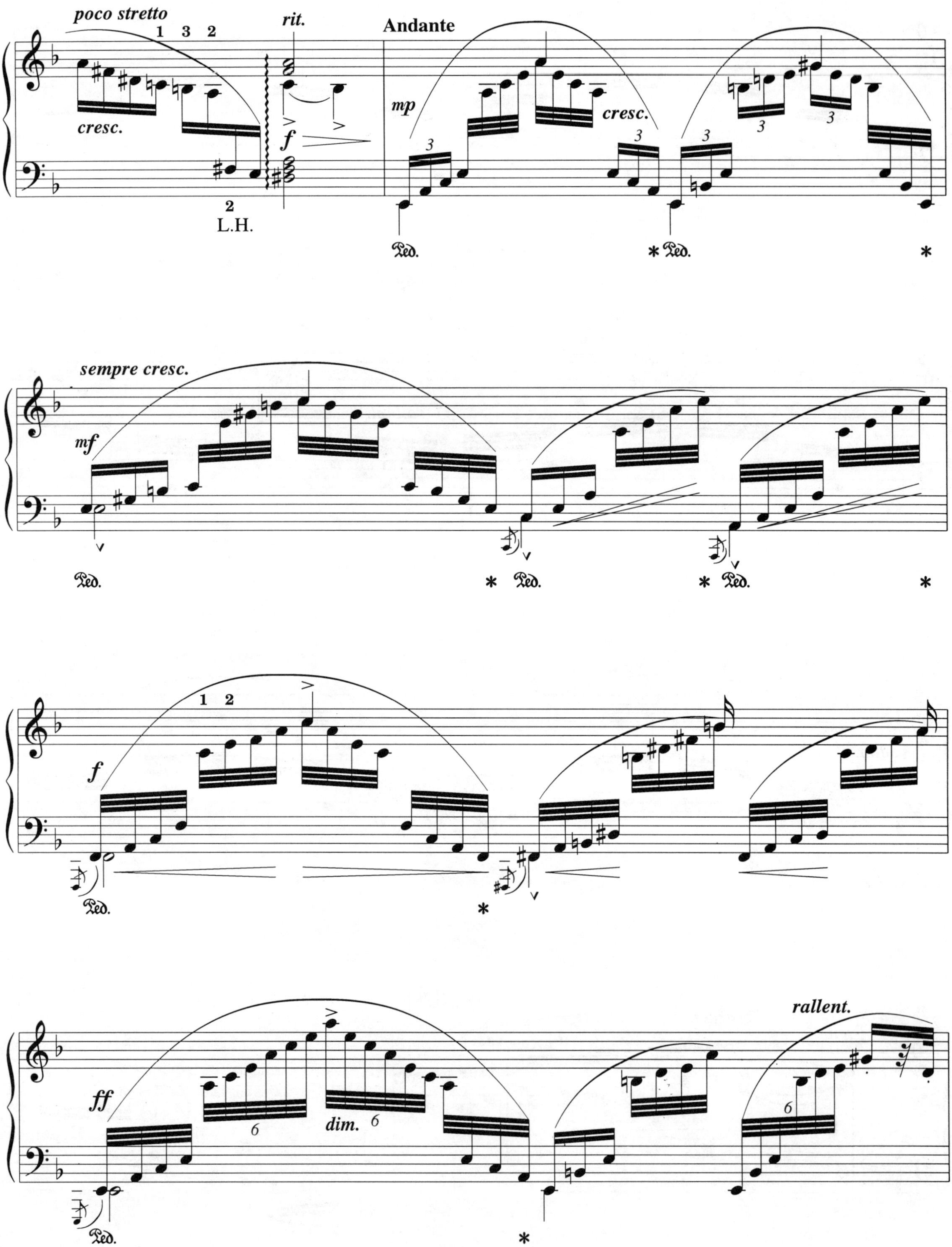
poco stretto
rit.
Andante
cresc.
mp
L.H.
Ped.
sempre cresc.
mf
f
ff
dim.
rallent.

Molto adagio
espress.
recit.
poco stretto
sfz
p
f
più lento
p espress.
poco stretto
mf
ten.
fz
p mf riten.
pp cresc.
Ped.

animato
mf
fz
p
largo pensieroso
pp
pp
accel.
Allegro
Adagio
molto espress.
mf
ten.
p
stretto
Andante
ten.
espress.
fz
ten.
f
più animato
L.H.
Allegro
f

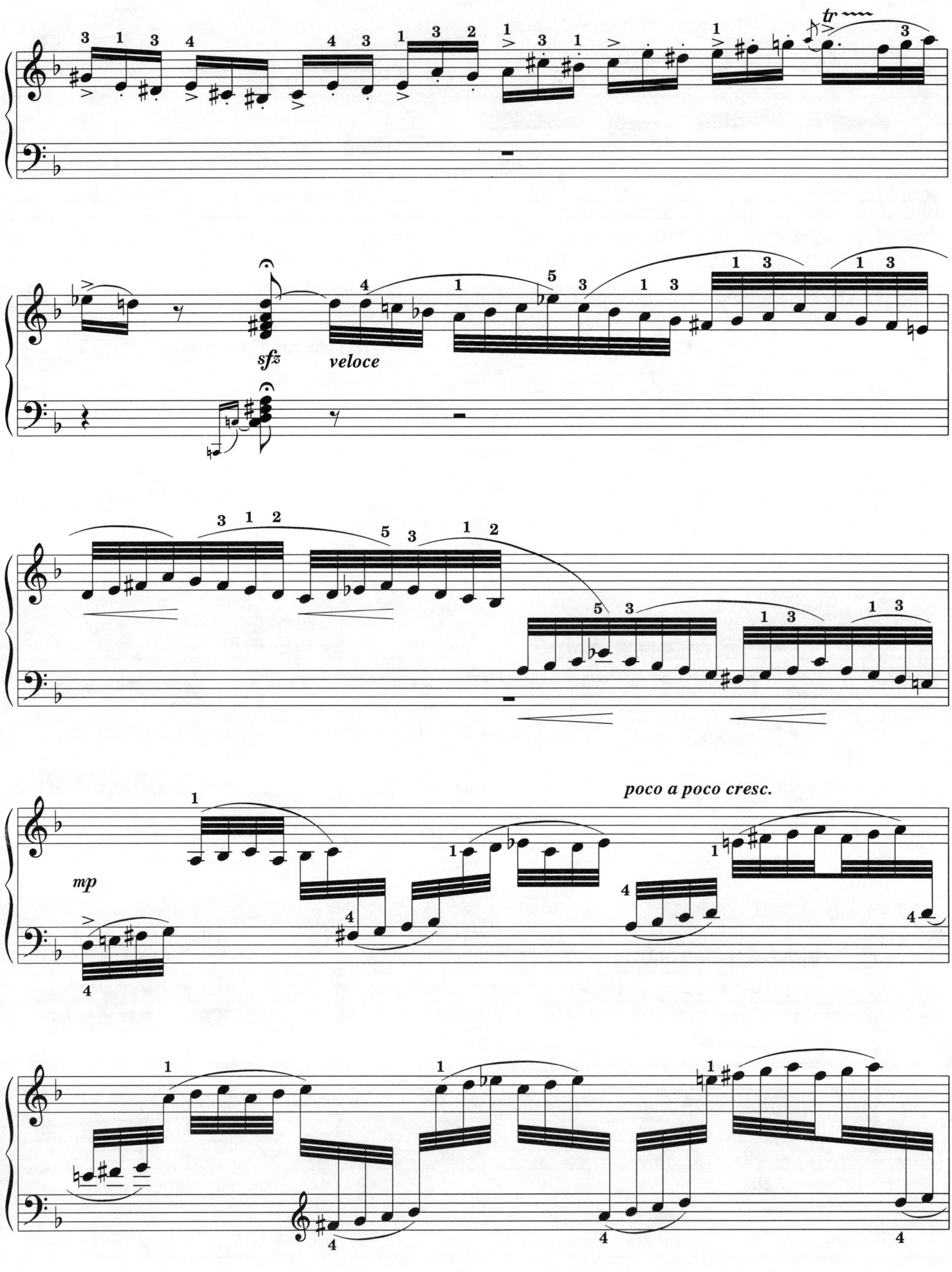
sfz
veloce
mp
poco a poco cresc.

cresc.
largamente
rapido
f
sfz
f
ten.
tr
riten. p
ten.
accel.
Adagio
mf
espress.
p
f
Ped.
Allegro
ten.
ff
ff
fz
Ped.

rallent.
decresc.
cresc.
pesante
fz
f
mf animato
poco rallent.
Maestoso
mf
ff
Lento rubato, quasi improvvisato
ten.
espress.
p

più lento
p
mf
f
pp dolciss.
ten.
poco a poco cresc. ed accel.
p
mf
ten.
f
fz
ten.
Maestoso
sfz ff
Adagio
tr
poco cresc.
pp
dim.
pp
ten.
pp
attacca la Fuga

Fugue

Poco allegro e tranquillo

ten.
p marcato
p
sempre piano
ten.
tr
tr
ten.
p e tranquillo
ten.
ten.
ten.
ten.
poco cresc.

ten.
ten.
ten.
dim.
p
poco riten.
tr
a tempo
ten.
mf
p
mf
ten.

p
mf
p
mf
p
p
ten.
ten.
ten.
ten.
p

tr
p
poco a poco cresc.
poco a poco animando il tempo sin'al Fine
f energico
sf
tr
sfz
sf
dim.
ten.

p
tr
mf
p
mf
ten.
marcato
mf
ten.
mf

tr
ten.
espress.
dim.
legato

molto cresc.
ffz dim.
ten.
p
mf
ten.
p
mf
p
cresc.
mf
tr
fp
f
p
tr
cresc.
f marcato

tr
ten.
fz
fz
p
ten.
35
p
p
cresc.
mf
p
p

cresc.
ten.
espress.
mf marcato
ten.
mf cresc. marcato

ff sostenuto e pesante
R.H.

cresc.
mf
cresc.
ff riten.
martellato
lunga
fff veloce
molto cresc.
Adagio
fz
fff

Robert Alexander Schumann

(June 8, 1810 – July 1856)

Robert Alexander Schumann was born on June 8, 1810, in the quaint little town of Zwickau, Germany. His father was a bookseller and publisher. Schumann was the youngest of five children.

At the age of nine he attended a concert by the famous pianist of the time, Moscheles. Hearing this concert artist inspired the young Schumann to play the piano and he began a little orchestra with his friends and filled in on the piano and composed pieces for this band. He amazed his father who then wrote to Carl Maria von Weber about teaching his son. Weber consented but nothing ever came of it, and then Schumann's father died in 1825.

His mother didn't share his enthusiasm for music and was determined that her son would be a lawyer. She sent him off to law school. After several frustrating and unhappy years, Robert Schumann, through the help of Friedrich Wieck — one of the best teachers in Germany and whose opinion Schumann's mother respected — was able to get his mother's consent to begin the study of music.

Trying to make up for lost time, Schumann invented a mechanical process to put his hand in condition, but instead, the excessive physical strain resulted in permanent injury to his right hand. Lessons with Wieck had to cease. This was indeed a discouraging incident. Deprived of a career as a pianist, he put his energy and talents into becoming a composer.

Schumann also became the editor of a musical guild that published a paper with musical criticism. Schumann stated the purpose of the journal to be to honor the old, to welcome the new, to denounce whatever was untrue to art, to proclaim anything that was worthy no matter from what source it came, to elevate the national taste by national art. "We write," he said, "not to enrich the tradesman but to honor the artist." Among the significant ones they advocated were: Schubert, Mendelssohn, Chopin, Gade, and Brahms.

While in the household of his teacher, Schumann had fallen in love with Friedrich Wieck's talented, charming daughter Clara. A tumultuous courtship went on for years, with Clara's father objecting to even letter correspondence. He didn't want anybody to interfere with his plans for Clara's concert career. Clara performed Robert Schumann's music at her concerts. They wrote secretly to each other and vowed to play the same song at the same hour to be "together" in spirit. Wieck had protested their ever dating and even threatened to kill Schumann.

Clara's mother, who had long been divorced from Wieck, consented to their wedding. On August 1, 1840, after six long years of waiting, their marriage was sanctioned by a court decree and on September 12, the day before Clara's twenty-first birthday, the wedding took place at the country church near Leipzig.

Music now poured from Schumann's happy heart. Within his first year of marriage he composed the Spring Symphony and the Piano Concerto in A Minor. Soon after the birth of their first child (the first of eight), Grandpa Wieck apologized and visited the couple for a reconciliation.

This "ideal" marriage did have its ups and downs. Clara's eminence as a concert artist compelled her to keep up her tours, but while she was away, Robert found it impossible to compose. When she returned, he immediately was inspired by her presence and could begin composing again.

To the general public Robert Schumann was "the husband" of Clara Wieck rather than the famous composer we think of today. Robert wrote abundantly for the piano. He wrote numerous easier pieces for his own children and very difficult compositions for his wife to perform.

Robert Schumann died July 1856, and he was buried in Bonn, Germany.

Papillons
(Op.2)

Robert Schumann

2

3

1.
2.
simile
sf
sf
1.
2.
ff
ff
4
4
p

4
Vivace
p
sf
cresc.
f
1.
2.
p
accel.
A tempo
cresc.
pp
accel.
cresc.
riten.
A tempo
p
sf
cresc.
ff

5
Allegretto
p
basso cantando
sf
sf
sf

8va
(8va)

6

sf
pp
mf leggiero
1.
2.
sf
sf
ff
sf

7

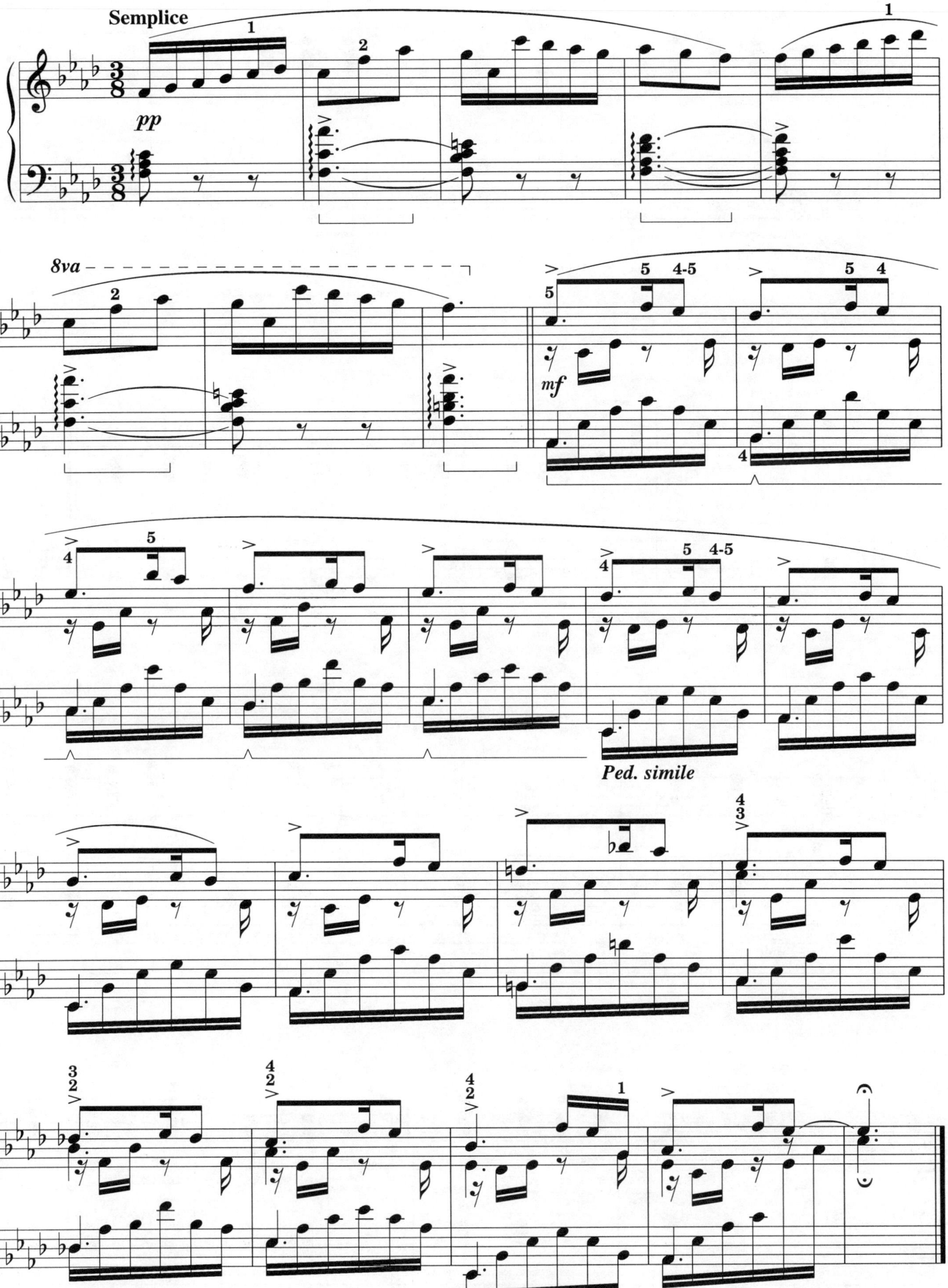

8

poco riten
f
A tempo
4
riten.

Presto
9
mf
sf
1.
2.
pp
sempre stacc.
stacc.

10
Vivo
pp
cresc.
Più lento
ff
p
simile

1.
2.
dim.
dim.
mf
pp
rit.
(una corda)
a tempo
p
(tre corde)
simile

mf
dim.
ff
p
rit.
pp

Allegro con spirito
11
sf
p
accel.
poco rit.
mf
f

8va
accel. e scherz.
(a tempo)

Più lento
8va
p
sempre legato
simile
sf
f
p
p molto legato
riten.
Ped. simile
Tempo primo
mf
sf

f
8va
ff
mf
f
p
pp

Finale
Allegro
12
f
1.
2.
mf
Tempo primo
Più lento
8va

8va
poco rit.
mf
sfz
Ped. sempre
poco a poco dim.

pp
p
(senza Ped.)
pp
ritard.
ppp
vivo

Johannes Brahms

(May 7, 1833 - April 3, 1897)

Brahms was a confirmed bachelor, very simple and down to earth. When he later became rich and famous, he remained a lodger in furnished rooms. Probably there was never a career less eventful than his. Brahms arose every day at five a.m., then brewed his early morning coffee himself because nobody else made it strong enough for his taste.

It is interesting to note that Brahms became a good friend of Robert Schumann, who used his influence to help Brahms get his first songs published .... which just happened to be piano pieces he had composed for the children of Robert and Clara Schumann.

Rhapsodie in G Minor

(Op. 79, No. 2)

Johannes Brahms

Molto passionato, ma non troppo allegro

legato
molto rit.
mp
a tempo
(senza Ped.)
più agitato
cresc.
f
riten.
p a tempo
misterioso
due corde
tre corde

crescendo
marcato
Ped.
*
1 1
f
8va
rit.
a tempo
L.H.
4
2
5
3

p espressivo
ritard.
L.H.
p
a tempo
L.H.
L.H.
L.H.
L.H.
L.H.
p
rit.

a tempo
due corde
R.H.
L.H.
rit.
p
a tempo
sempre due corde
Ped.
misterioso
P
tre corde
ff
poco rit.

a tempo
ff
p
dim.
Ped.
rit.
ppp
sotto voce
a tempo
L.H.
due corde
L.H.
L.H.
L.H.
L.H.
L.H.
L.H.
(R.H.)
poco rit.

L.H.
a tempo
tre corde
ff
p
(L.H.)
pp
due corde
accel.
dim. ritenuto

a tempo
lunga
tre corde
L.H.
L.H.
rit.
a tmpo
L.H.
L.H.
rit.
a tmpo

malto rit.
mp
a tempo
(senza)
cresc.
f
riten.
p a tempo
due corde

Grandioso
f
cresc.
tre corde
marcato
ff pesante
ff
p
dim.
quasi rit.
T.S.P.
pp
smorzando
ppp
ff

Jakob Ludwig Felix Mendelssohn

(November 3, 1809 - November 4, 1847)

As a composer, a man, a friend, with society and family Mendelssohn stands apart. He was a man of taste and integrity. Mendelssohn's favorite motto was: "What is worth doing at all is worth doing well."

He was born November 3, 1809, in Hamburg, Germany. His father was a rich banker. His mother spoke several languages, read Homer in the original, and played the piano. When Mendelssohn was three years old, the French captured the city and the family fled to Berlin. A new banking house was established. The whole family were baptized into the Lutheran Church and adopted the additional name of Bartholdy. They lived in a beautiful home with gardens and a big tree lined canal in front of their home. All distinguished musical people who passed through Berlin visited the Mendelssohns.

When Mendelssohn was almost ten years old, he made his first public appearance as a pianist. He was very well received. From this time on he began to compose. There were sonatas, songs, a cantata, and sixty movements in 1821. He wrote or copied them with the greatest neatness and care in volumes which by the end of his life extended to forty-four in number and are now preserved in the Berlin Library. He always played his pieces from memory. On Sunday at the Mendelssohn home there was always an afternoon concert by Felix and Fanny and sometimes other musicians of Berlin.

Professor Zelter became Mendelssohn's master teacher. Mendelssohn's father Abraham had presented Zelter with a quantity of cantatas and other manuscripts by "the poor Cantor of Leipzig." Zelter reverenced these pieces by J. S. Bach and sometimes took Mendelssohn up to the closet of the Singakademie where they were stored, but he never allowed Mendelssohn to touch them. At last Mendelssohn's grandmother obtained a copy of the score of Bach's Passion Music and presented it to him Christmas 1823. This had great influence on him. He formed a small choir and rehearsals began January 1828, and the work was performed publicly on March 11, 1829, for the first time since the death of its composer. The apathy of the people which he dreaded was stirred to enthusiasm. Every ticket was sold and hundreds were turned away. This was the beginning of the Bach revival.

Mendelssohn found time not only to compose, but also for watercolor painting, swimming, dancing, billiards, chess, and riding. He spent half a year in Rome and was fortunate enough to witness the coronation of a pope. Mendelssohn spent six weeks in Naples, then visited Florence, Genoa, and Milan. From Geneva he walked to Interlachen, where he composed his only waltzes. Mendelssohn went to Paris, then to London where he gave four concerts. After the musical season was over he went to Scotland, stopping at the Hebrides where he was inspired to compose his overture called "Fingal's Cave".

After all his trips Mendelssohn had to stay in London for two more months recuperating in his room with a lame knee. It prevented him from being present at his sister Fanny's wedding.

In March 1837, at Frankfurt, he married his beautiful sweetheart Cecile Charlotte Sophie Jeanrenaud. Shortly after their honeymoon, Mendelssohn had to go to England for his fifth trip to conduct his music at the Birmingham Festival. In one letter to his wife he said, "What is the good of all the double counterpoint in the world, if Cecile is not with me?"

Ever since 1838 Mendelssohn had kept in mind the subject of Elijah for an oratorio. In the midst of his incessant labors as head of the Conservatorium, teaching piano, composition and overseeing administrative details, Felix managed to finish the oratorio in time for the Birmingham Festival of 1846. While in London he played two hours at Buckingham Palace for the Queen and the Prince Consort alone.

This visit was his tenth to London and upon returning home Mendelssohn found out his sister had died. With a cry, he fell to the ground unconscious. He spent the entire summer in Switzerland resting and painting in watercolors. Thirteen large pictures of Swiss scenery are in existence. When Mendelssohn returned home his friends were shocked at how depressed he seemed and how much he had aged!

Felix Mendelssohn died November 4, 1847. All Europe mourned. Scholarships were established in his honor. Busts and statues of him were also erected.

Variations Sérieuses

(Op. 54)

Felix Mendelssohn
Composed in 1841

sf
dim.
sf
sf
p
sf
sf
sf
p
ten.
sf
f
dim.
p

Var. 2

Un poco più animato

Var. 3
Più animato
p
crescendo
f
p
crescendo
f
sf
p
f
sf
f
sf
p
f
sf
piu f
sf
ff

Var. 4

fp sempre stacc. e leggero
Ped simile
cresc.
dim.
crescendo
Ped simile
f
cresc.
ff
dim.
p

Var. 5

Agitato
p legato ed espressivo
dim.
Ped. simile

cresc.
sf
sf
espressivo
p rit.
Var. 6
a tempo
cresc.
p crescendo
Ped. simile
sempre più f
f
sf
sf
sf
Ped. simile
sempre ff
sf
ff
ff

Var. 7

Var. 8

Allegro vivace

Var. 9
sf
crescendo
sf
sf
sf
f
f
sf
p
f
sf
p
f
ff
sf

sf
f
Ped. simile
ff
Var. 10
Moderato
mf
p
crescendo
cresc.
dim.
rit.

Var. 11
cantabile
pp
Ped. simile
crescendo
p
crescendo
ritardando al forte
sf
f
Var. 12
sf
f Tempo del Tema
sf
sf sempre
Ped. simile
f
sf

sf
sf
f
sf
sf
sf
f
cresc.
ff
sf

Var.13

Var. 14
Adagio
mf
p
p
cresc.
f
dim.
ritard.
p
Var. 15
poco a poco più agitato
sempre
pp
Ped. simile
cresc.
sf
dim.

Var. 16

Var. 17

ff
sf
Ped. ten.
sf ff
Ped. ten.
8va
mf
sf
ritenuto
sf
sf
accel.
cresc.

rit.
Presto
cresc.
Ped. simile

cresc.
f
f
cresc.
Ped. simile
sf
cresc.
sf
cresc.
sf
sf
ffz
ffz
ffz

ffz
ffz
ffz
ffz
ffz
ffz
sfz
Ped. ten.
legato
sempre ff
8va
dim.
p

Frederic Francois Chopin

(February 22, 1809 – October 17, 1849)

Chopin's father was a French teacher. His mother was Polish. His boyhood summers were spent in the country where he heard the music of the peasants and danced the national Kujawiak. At the age of 18, his father sent him to Berlin to meet musicians and hear the music performed there. When Chopin returned to Warsaw he composed two piano concertos. Soon Chopin decided to leave home for Paris. Friends went with him to a banquet in a neighboring village and there presented him with a silver cup filled to the brim with Polish soil. They solemnly asked him never to forget friends and fatherland. When Chopin arrived in Paris, he was somewhat unknown and through the kindness of Franz Liszt — who got an immense satisfaction from discovering talent — was introduced into Parisian society. Chopin played at the house of Baron Jocob Rothchild one evening and that was the beginning of his great popularity! Soon "Opus Two" was published and the critique that Robert Schumann gave in his German musical publication was, "Hats off, gentlemen: a genius!"

Chopin told Schumann that he had been "incited to the creation of the Ballades" by the poetry of his compatriot Adam Mickiewicz. Chopin said that the G minor Ballade was suggested by the poem Konrad Wallrod. Schumann thought that the G minor Ballad, Opus 23, was "the most spirited, most daring work of Chopin."

Premiére Ballade

(Op. 23)

Frédéric Chopin

* In some editions: 

riten.
agitato

sempre più mosso
8va
più f
(8va)
poco a poco meno f

8va
(8va)
calando
smorz.
dim. e riten.
Ped.

Meno mosso
sotto voce
pp
pp sempre

sempre
dim. e rallent.
R.H.
a tempo
sotto voce
R.H.

p
cresc.
fz
pp
cresc.
fz
sempre cresc.
fz
fz
rit.
molto cresc.
a tempo
ff
Ped.

Ped.
ff
8va

ffz
dim.
p
cresc.

8va
(8va)
(8va)
p
Ped.
*

cresc.
ff

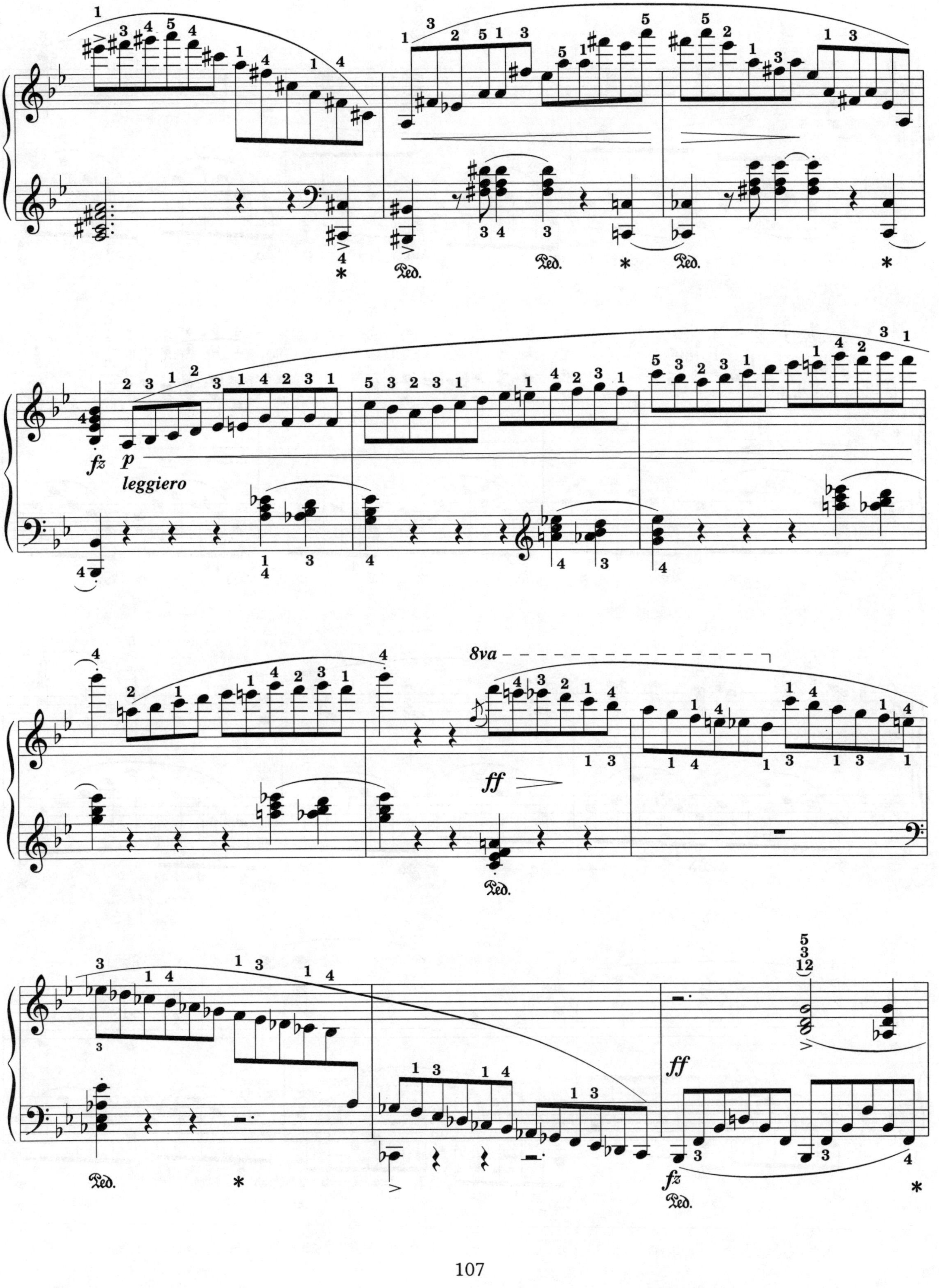
fz
p
leggiero
8va
ff
Ped.

tr
ten.
con forza
ten.
f sempre
Ped.

riten.
dim. rall.
Meno mosso
pp sempre
sotto voce
cresc.
fz
p
cresc.
fz
Ped.

fz
molto cresc.
8va
il più forte possibile
Presto con fuoco
ff

cresc.
8va
ff
(8va)

mf
cresc.
8va
fz
Ped.

fz
p riten.
f accel.
fz
8va
(8va)
f
p riten.
f accel.
8va
fff poco ritenuto
accel.
Ped.

Fantaisie - Impromptu

(Op. 66)

Posthumous
Frédéric Chopin

cresc.
dim.
f
p
cresc.
f

pp
riten.
a tempo
p
8va
cresc.

sempre cresc.
f
8va
ff
riten.

Largo
pesante
Moderato cantabile
sotto voce
rit.
a tempo

tr
sf
tr
sf
f
pp
tr
sf
tr

tr
sf
7
f
tr
3
tr
riten.

Presto
p
8va
cresc.
dim.

f
p
cresc.
f

pp
riten.
a tempo
p
8va
cresc.
sempre cresc.

f
8va
ff

sempre f
(dim.)
p
f
(dim.)
p
f
poco a poco dim.

p
pp
il canto marcato
riten.
ppp

Sigismund Thalberg

(1812–1871)

Sigismund Thalberg was born in 1812 in Austria. He was the son of Prince Moritz Dietrichstein and Baroness von Wetzlar. Thalberg was a student of Hummel and Kalkbrenner. At the age of 13, Thalberg was already playing at private parties in Vienna. In 1830, following the publication of three of his works, Thalberg went on his first concert tour through Germany. In 1834 Thalberg was appointed Kammervirtuoso to the Emperor of Austria.

Thalberg was one of the most outstanding pianists of the 19th Century. A characteristic of his music creates the illusion of three hands at the keyboard! This effect was accomplished by dividing the melody between the two hands so that a bass could be played with the left hand and the accompaniment with the right hand, giving the sound of three independent hands. Almost 30 of his piano works are operatic fantasias.

In 1843, Sigismund Thalberg married Mme. Boucher, the widow of a famous painter, in Paris. Thalberg was an idolized figure the world over. He gave numerous European concert tours and was considered a rival of Franz Liszt. In 1857 he visited the United States. Then, in 1863 Thalberg retired as a pianist and moved to Brazil, becoming a vintner. Sigismund Thalberg died April 27, 1871, in Posilipo, which is near Naples.

Les Huguenots
(Op. 20)

S. Thalberg

p
f
f
ff
pesante
ritard.
A tempo
p
leggiero
8va
p
p
8va
8va
8va
8va
8va

8va
8va
8va
8va
8va
8va
8va
8va
8va
8va
p
ritard.
leggiero
p

lunga pausa
Andante con espressione
p

cresc.
f
dim.
perdendosi
legatissimo
12

cresc.
cresc.
p
con grasia
dim.
3
12
8va
ritard.
12/8

Listesso tempo
p
agitato
cresc.
sempre
cresc.
f
p
(tr)
f
p
tr
Ped.

Ped.
*
Ped.
*
dim.
Ped.
*
Ped.
*
cresc.
A tempo
f
ritenuto
f
ff
dim.
p
cresc.
ff
dim.
cresc.

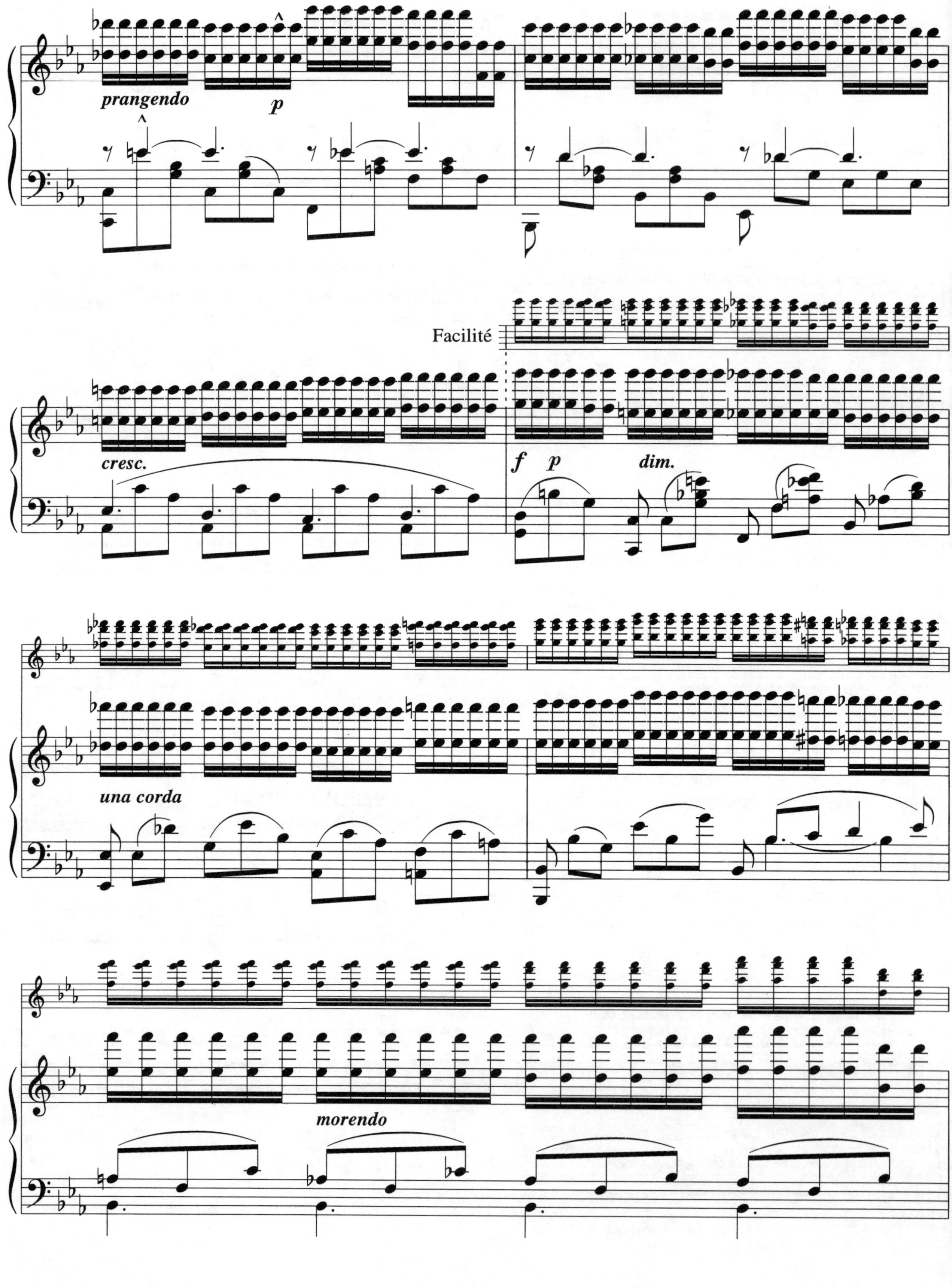
prangendo
p
Facilité
cresc.
f
p
dim.
una corda
morendo

A tempo
p
cresc.
8va
f
p

8va
8va

8va
p
p
cresc.
f
dim.
p
cresc.

f
dim.
p
legato
ritard.
Largo
p
Choral
una corda
Religioso
con tutta la forza
ff

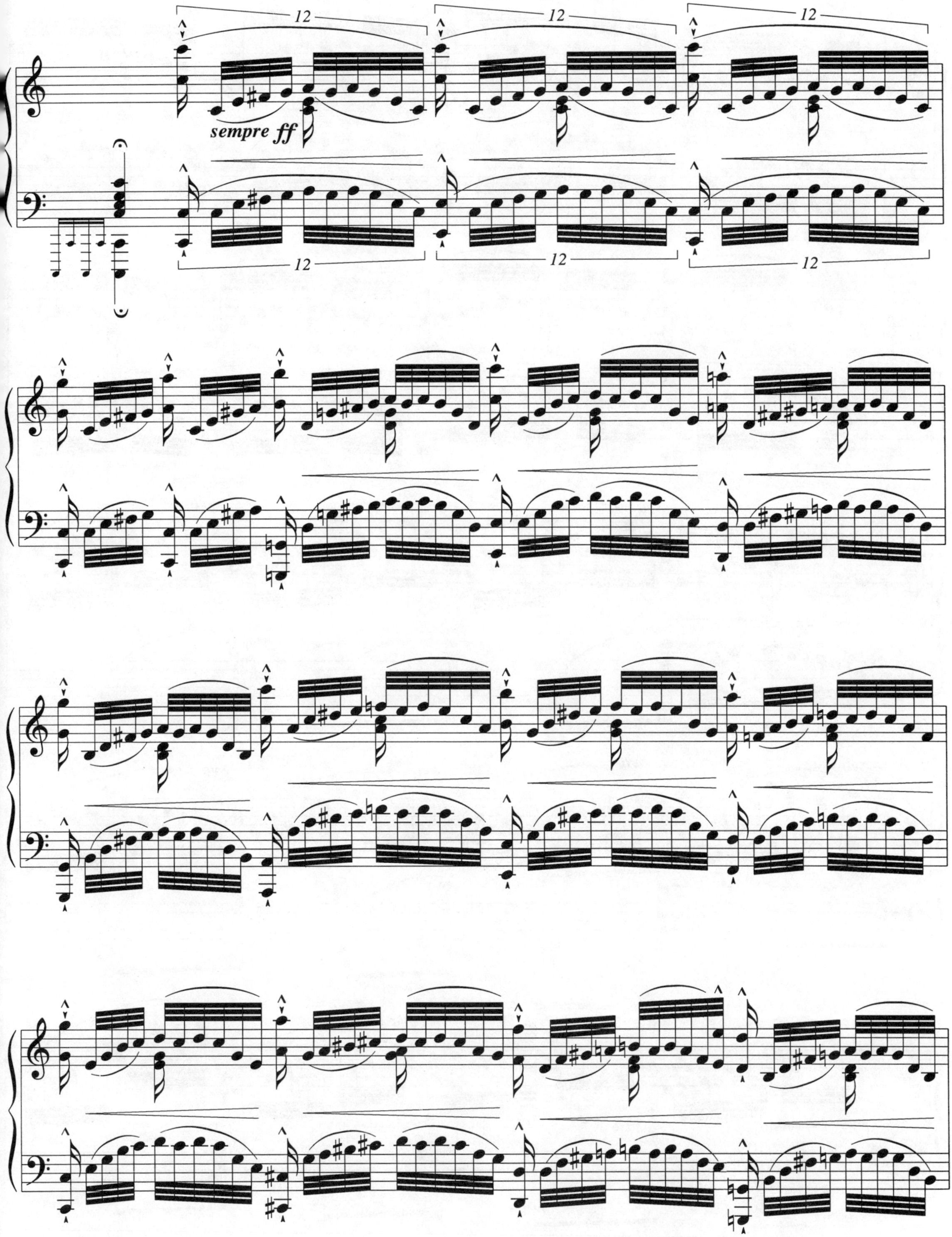
12
12
12
sempre ff
12
12
12

8va
p
f

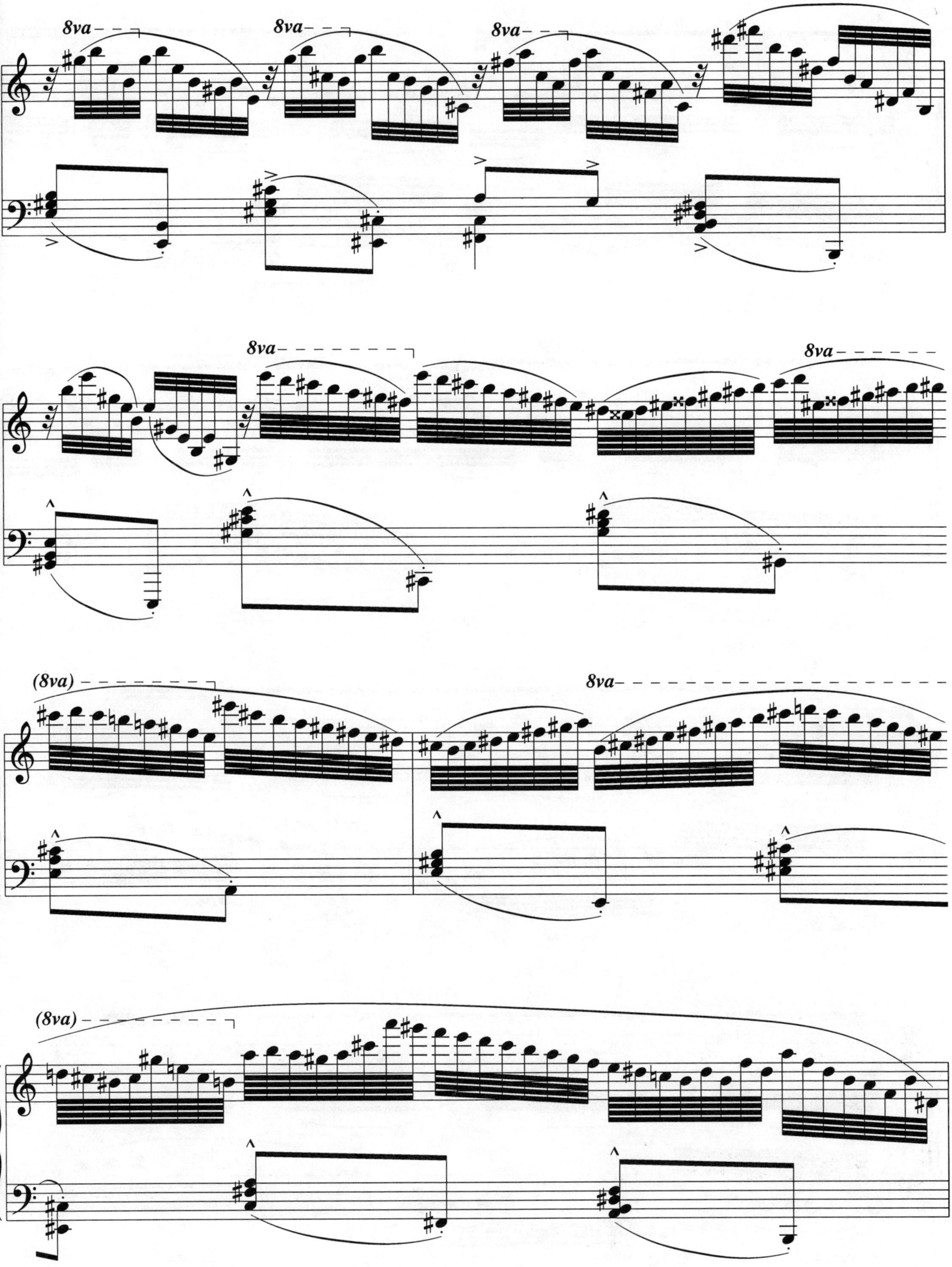
8va
8va
8va
8va
8va
(8va)
8va
(8va)

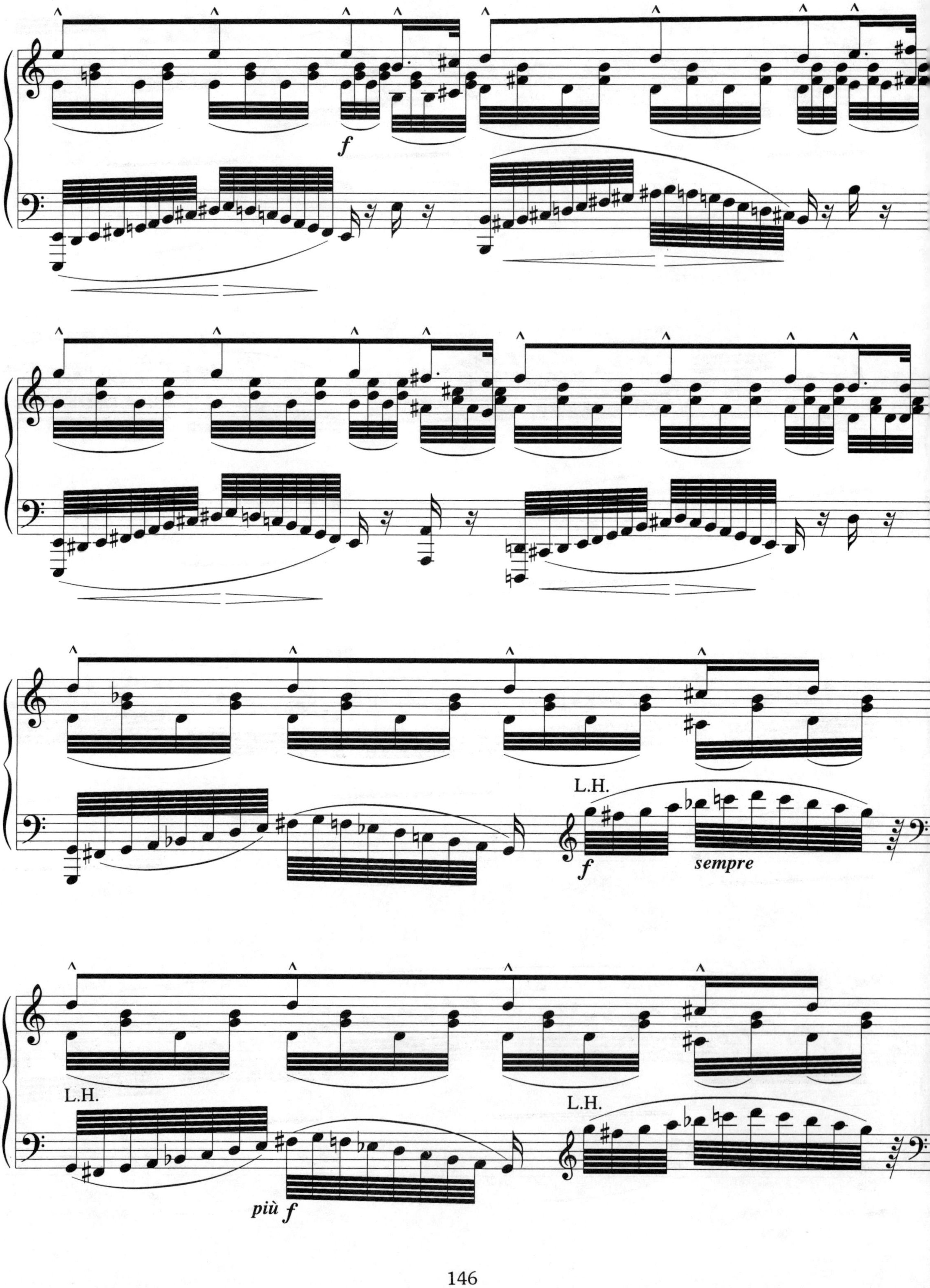
f
L.H.
f
sempre
L.H.
più f
L.H.

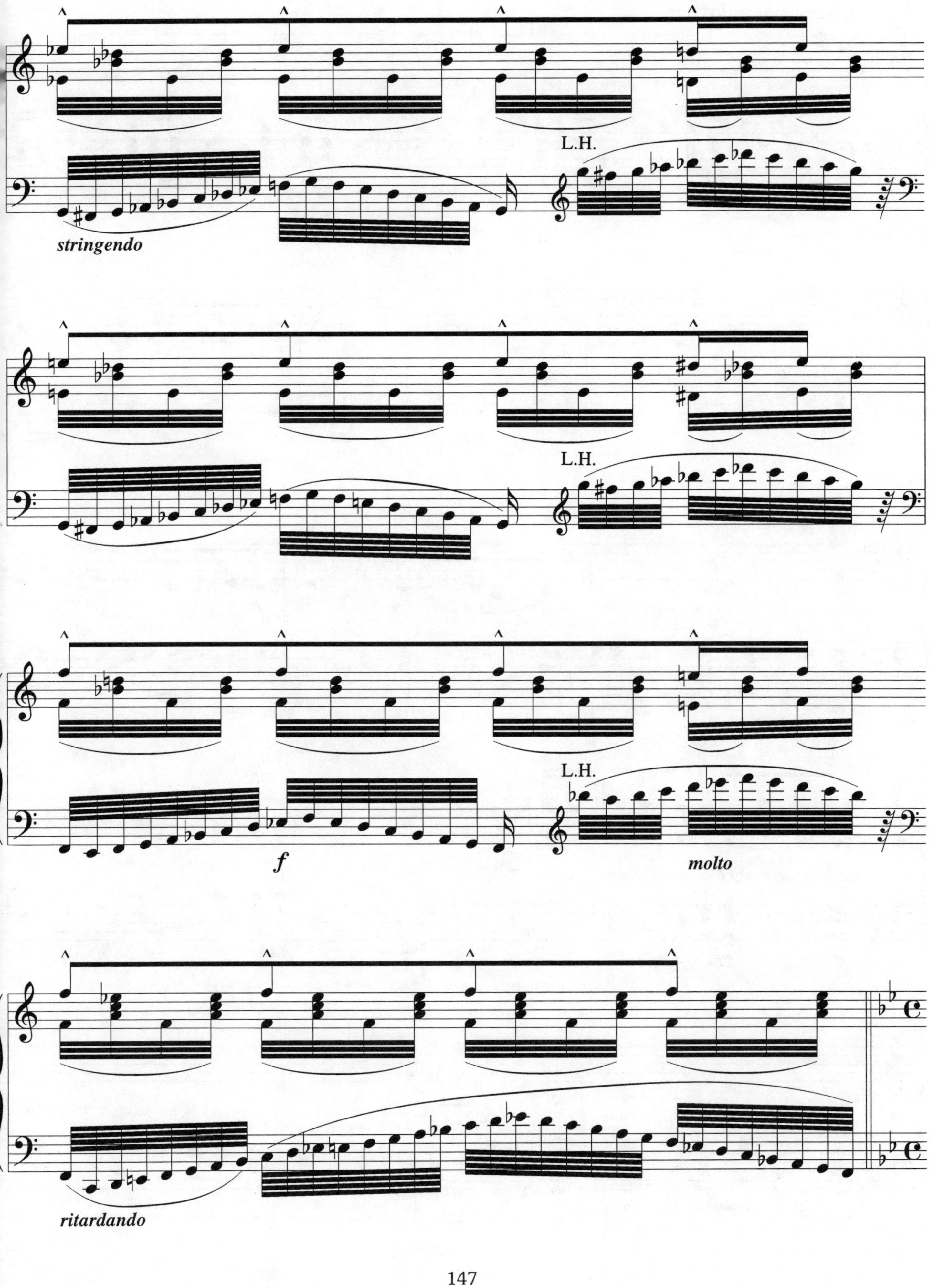
L.H.
stringendo
L.H.
L.H.
f
molto
ritardando

Allegro moderato
p
p
f
ff
f
f
f
p
ff

una corda
ff
pp
f
dim.
Allegretto
ff

p
f
p
f
f
dim.
p

f
ff
p
legato

f
p
8va
leggierissimo
8va
8va
8va

8va
8va
8va
pp
8va
p
8va
p
scherzando
p
8va

8va
sempre p
8va
8va
p
cresc.
8va
strepito

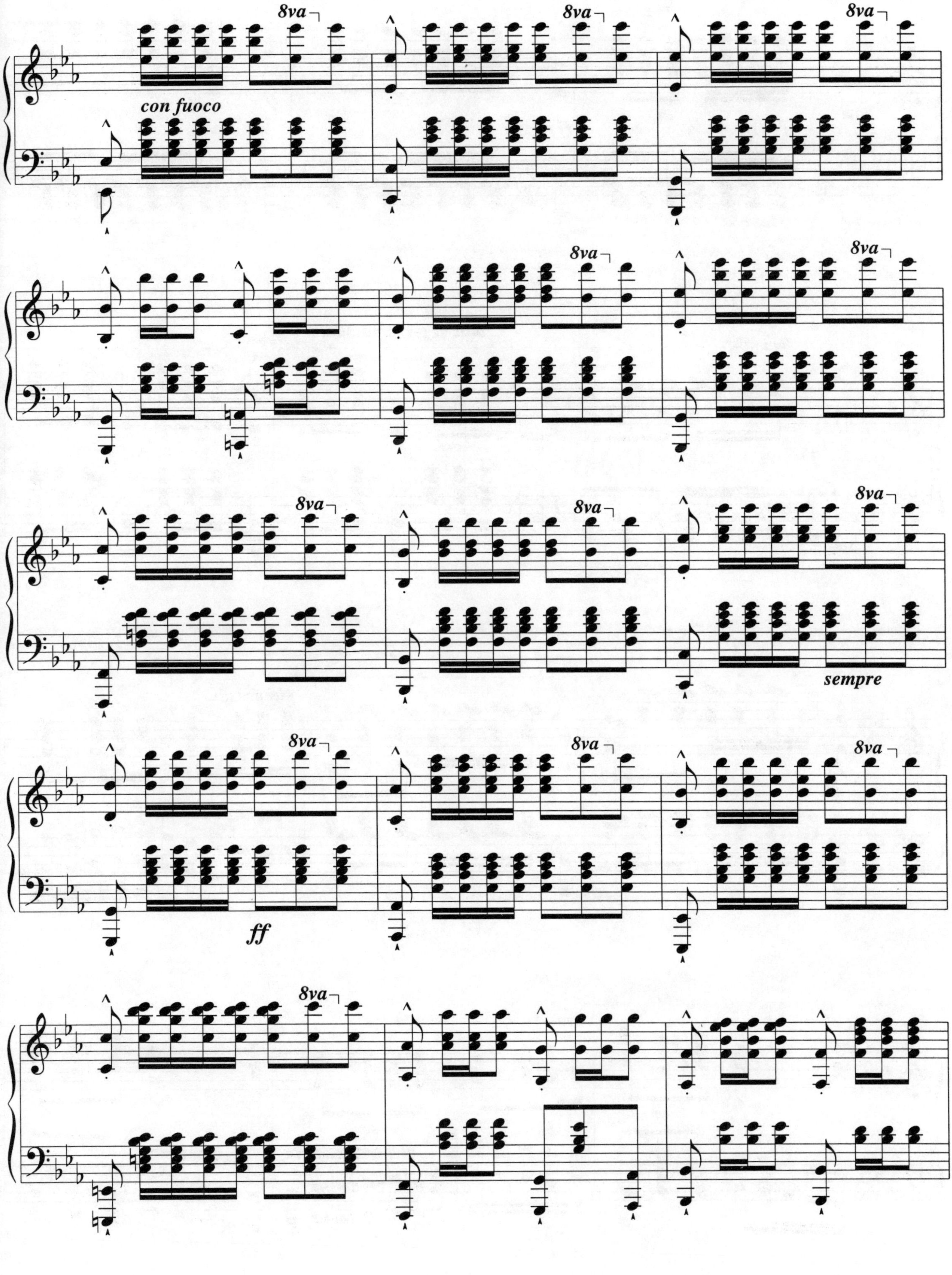
con fuoco
8va
sempre
ff

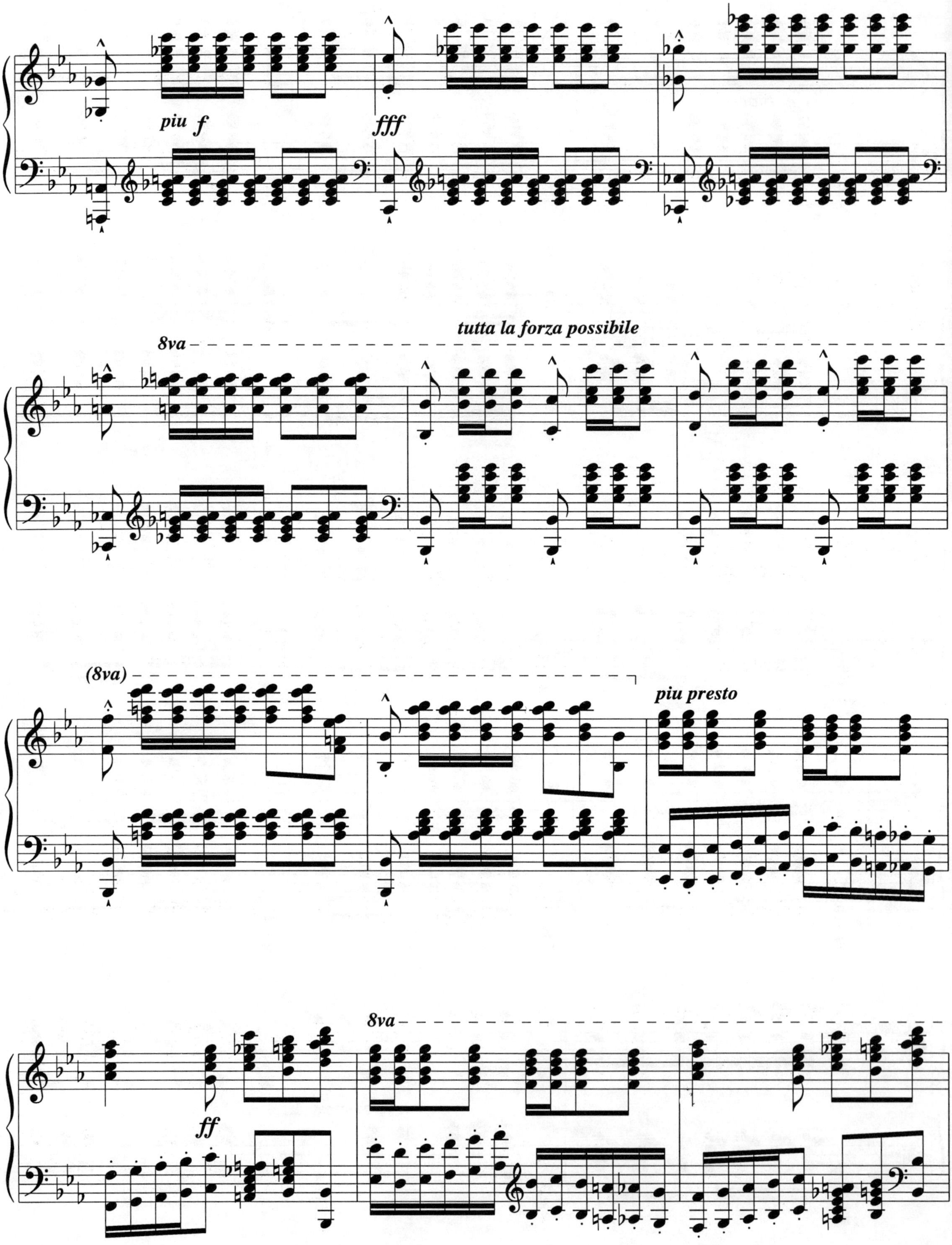
piu f
fff
8va
tutta la forza possibile
(8va)
piu presto
ff
8va

(8va)
8va
8va
8va
ff
fff